Mrs. Howard
Room by Room

THE ESSENTIALS OF DECORATING
· WITH SOUTHERN STYLE

PHOEBE HOWARD

WRITTEN WITH MARC KRISTAL

STEWART, TABORI & CHANG | NEW YORK

DEDICATION

$\mathcal{I}$ dedicate this book to my incredible mother, Madeline McGinty. She is the most intelligent, free-spirited, talented, and courageous person I have ever known. Somehow she managed to raise me to be confident and strong, and to trust my instincts. She is the single person responsible for my drive and strong work ethic. I was raised with the perfect balance of structure and freedom, and my mother taught me to be fearless: to go for it.

Lucky for me she was retiring when we first started the stores, and she is an integral part of our business success. She is the reason I was able to raise a family and start a business. Whenever I needed to travel, she would just move in our house with our kids, who always loved being with their granny. My children are closer to her in many ways than they are to me. When Jim and I would leave on antique buying trips, she would always appear with a bag that contained two tomato sandwiches, honestly the best thing you have ever tasted. Jim and I took off on many adventures with the juice of a tomato sandwich dripping from our chins, and we will never forget them.

My mother is beautiful, glamorous, funny, and whip smart. She has the true soul of an artist and more talent than anyone deserves. She was an art teacher for most of my childhood, and instead of plastic toys, we played with clay and glazes, with paint and paper, or something to carve: wood or stone. I always marveled at whatever she was making as we sat together countless nights creating something as a family: my mom and my four brothers. I have spent my life chasing her elusive talent, and I would be completely satisfied with a tiny fraction of her gifts. Mom, I love you and thank you for all you have done for me. This book is for you.

INTRODUCTION
page 6

FOYERS
page 10

LIVING ROOMS
page 30

LIBRARIES
page 144

MASTER BEDROOMS
page 166

GUEST ROOMS
page 194

DINING ROOMS
page 58

KITCHENS
page 80

FAMILY ROOMS
page 114

KIDS' ROOMS
page 216

BATHROOMS
page 236

OUTDOORS
page 254

INTRODUCTION

Design is little more than an opinion. You could ask ten different designers to tell you what their vision is for a room, and you would get ten different answers. Everyone has their own point of view regarding how a room should be put together. No one is right, or wrong, because decorating is subjective. My decorating is a representation of my opinion of how rooms should look and feel. When starting a new project, I ask for as much input as possible from my clients and look for clues. How will they use the house? How do they want it to feel? How does it need to function? What styles, colors, and arrangements do they prefer? Ultimately it is my job to assemble all of the various items my clients select and create an environment for them that is not only a reflection of their style and taste but also suitable for and specifically tailored to their needs. Throughout the entire process I offer my opinion regarding which pieces, colors, patterns, and textures should be selected, and the reasons why I feel that way. The most valuable asset I can offer my clients is my experience, my years and years of decorating houses. This is something not to be overlooked, because with each new project you will learn something new, not only about decorating, but also about yourself and your own creativity.

This stately Southern home is anchored by a beautiful mantel and a painting by Isabelle Melchior. The layering of creams and grays creates a soft contrast with the colorful artwork.

I have chosen to break the challenge of decoration into easy-to-manage parts. Decorating room by room is not only easier, it is also a great way to build confidence and define your own style.

Decorating a house, or even a room, is an overwhelming process for most people. There are so many elements that come into play when assembling a room, let alone an entire house. In this book, I thought it might be helpful if I addressed rooms rather than houses. What makes a living room great? How should I lay out my kitchen? How can I make our family room really comfortable? These are the types of questions that my clients and store customers ask me over and over again. In this book, I get into the details to try to break down the process of how to furnish a room. Even though most of my clients are wealthy people, it is my hope that, regardless of budget, some of these rules and ideas can apply to any house.

Decorating is a very detailed and layered process. So much thought and planning goes into it, much more than most people realize. We work on our projects for months and even years. This is where creativity takes a backseat and the real business of decorating begins. Not only do you have to plan for and select each item, you also have to order it, store it in a warehouse, safely deliver it in a truck, and install it in the house. We think about and work on our projects nonstop during the process and are always tweaking, adding, and refining our ideas. We go over it and over it again and again. When the day finally arrives to deliver the final product to our clients, it is literally like a drug to me. I can't sleep or eat the night before the big day. We watch as everything is carefully carried from the truck into the house, unwrapped, and placed. First come the rugs. Then the curtains and window coverings. Next the big pieces, the upholstery, the beds and tables and chairs. The art, the accessories, the lamps, the bedding all come trickling in. At every moment we are making sure that every item is correctly made, that the sizes are correct, that the finishes are right, and, of course, that nothing has been damaged along the way. This is a nerve-wracking process for any decorator. This is the moment of truth, when you get to see your and your client's vision become a reality. Layer by layer, bit by bit, it slowly unfolds before you. I find it an exhilarating process, but it is also one fraught with problems. Inevitably something will go wrong, and we have to quickly find a way to solve the problem.

The hardest part for me is finishing the job, thanking my clients, and walking away from the house. By the time a project is done, I have formed such a strong attachment to it that I have quite a bit of separation anxiety. I live and breathe these jobs. To turn the house over to my clients and know that I am moving on to the next job is always hard. I have been in daily contact with my clients during the entire process, and I know that I will miss them. And hopefully, they will miss me, too. (Or buy another house!) It brings me so much happiness and, yes, joy to know that I have met or even exceeded their expectations. I have been very lucky over the years and have worked with some incredible clients who not only trusted me, but also understood the importance of a professional collaboration.

Not unlike a wedding, when a project is over, all you have left are your memory and the photographs. The pictures in this book are what I can take with me, and look at over and over again, so I can keep the memory with me forever. In this book, I wanted to share these rooms with you and explain the process that went into creating them. Hopefully you can take something from these pages that will inspire you to create your own special rooms. Always keep in mind that decorating is a complicated process that takes time, planning, and money. It is an expensive undertaking, and it is easy to make costly mistakes. The more planning and thoughtful collaboration that you allow, the better the result will be. Be patient and take your time—it should not happen overnight. Let your house show who you are, what you like, and where you are going. And during that process, I sincerely hope you find your joy of decorating!

Foyers

$\mathcal{J}$im and I had been married about three years when we began stalking a house in our neighborhood. It was a Federal-style red brick house built in 1920. It had a beautiful half-round portico with Doric columns, and a stately six-panel door with a double-radius arched fanlight above, and flanking sidelights, all in a graceful leaded glass pattern. We drove past this house constantly, observed that someone elderly was living there, and noticed that there did not ever seem to be any activity. We finally worked up the nerve to knock on the door and ask if the house was for sale.

The lady of the house graciously invited us in. I will never forget that moment. There was a wide single hall with a central staircase. The foyer was flanked by a perfect pair of classical arches in the Federal style—with Colonial reeded casings terminating in keystones—that led into the dining room on the right and the living room on the left. At the end of the hall there was light streaming into the entire space and a beautiful view into the tree-lined backyard.

That house had us right at the front door. We literally made an offer right then and there in the foyer and never even looked at the rest of the house: not the kitchen, bathroom, upstairs, or anything else. As luck would have it, our timing was perfect, our offer was accepted, and we spent many happy years there with our family. On many occasions the stairs were draped with garland for the holidays, and numerous festive parties were held there. I dreamed of our two girls getting married in that house—it definitely had that *Father of the Bride* charm. Every time I threw open that door to greet a guest, I was so proud and excited to welcome them in. Eventually

PREVIOUS: *Jim designed this oval-shaped foyer, with its elegant stone floor, for a grand Southern home; I love the metallic wallpaper with its cascading leaves.* OPPOSITE: *I treated the curved walls of this Atlanta foyer with a high-gloss robin's-egg-blue finish that evokes melted glass, then added the four Venetian shell-shaped sconces and English hall chairs. I like the relationship between the compass pattern in the Italian center table and the "sun" pendant fixture above.*

we moved to a house on the water, so I never got to see a wedding there, but the time we spent there was so memorable. To this day we miss that house terribly.

Given how powerful an impact that foyer had on us, I think the space is very important—it's the part of your house in which to make a great first impression and set a positive tone for what is to come. As a result, even though you spend hardly any time in it—especially given the fact that most families enter or exit through the side or back door—the foyer is a real make-or-break experience.

And of course, you want your guests to look forward to visiting, which is why I treat the front porch as part of the arrival experience, the prelude to the entry. That means proper landscaping and lighting, a doormat that does not look worn, no cobwebs on the porch roof, and a front door with sparkling clean glass and polished brass. It does not take a lot of effort, but that kind of thoughtfulness and care really says something about you as a host—your friends will feel good about being there even before they have rung the bell.

You don't have a lot of elements with which to work, so furnishing a foyer is not that complicated. I usually choose overscaled pieces that make a statement, rather than a lot of small items that can make a foyer feel crowded or cluttered. The walls are the main event, and it is a great space in which to be playful with color or to try out a patterned wallpaper. A rug or runner warms up the space nicely and creates a decorative impact as well; I also favor gentle lamplight and a mirror in which to check yourself on the way in or out. If you have the room, a console table provides a place for keys and mail and a showcase for a few decorative objects. Since you won't have a lot of furniture there, think about layering your foyer, with a basket under the console or an umbrella stand by the front door. I also think it's nice to introduce a fragrance. Fresh flowers or greenery are my favorite way to breathe life into the space, but a scented candle will do almost as well.

The one thing to avoid is family photos: The foyer is about your guests and should express a certain public character. But try not to make it too formal or intimidating—whether you go for stunning and glamorous or low-key and simple, the ultimate goal is a space that is warm and welcoming.

I wanted this handsome Jacksonville foyer, in a 1920s Georgian-style house, to have a contemporary vitality, and so we engaged the Little Rock decorative painter Andrew Bruckman to create the patterned floor and added a leopard-patterned runner on the stair. The abstract painting by Cecil Touchon, paired playfully with an eighteenth-century "dolphin" console, further subtracts from the overall formality.

To glamorize the space, we lacquered all of the doors in the Jacksonville foyer a deep high-gloss black, pairing the color with brass hardware. The graduated alabaster pendant echoes the movement of the strong dentil molding. An antique Irish oval mirror hangs above a Biedermeier-style walnut commode.

16

THIS PAGE: *A rustic antique table is paired with a modern glass lamp and my client's antique camera. The photos are by Diane Arbus and André Kertész.*
OPPOSITE: *I found this wonderfully funky, Portuguese baroque-style settee on a trip to France and thought it would serve as an excellent foil for the photograph from my client's collection. The linen pull-up table and lamps complete the vignette.*

A foyer is a delicate balance: It should reflect your tastes and interests, but not get too personal for a "public" space of welcome.

THIS PAGE: *The light foyer opposite is followed by a dark gallery-like space in which my client's Sam Francis canvas shimmers against the deep navy wall. The bench, designed by Geoffrey Bradfield, is in the manner of Gilbert Poillerat.*
OPPOSITE: *In this sophisticated New York foyer, a patterned marble floor, fluted walls, and a cove ceiling finished in gold leaf showcase artworks by Roy Lichtenstein and a 1950s vintage bronze-and-marble console table by Jules Leleu.*

Great art makes a dazzling impact in a foyer, and I am grateful when a client presents interesting and varied artworks before the design process begins.

OPPOSITE: *This foyer, in a classic Southern home in Birmingham, incorporates a simple Chinese console and striped wallpaper.* THIS PAGE: *This large, light-filled foyer in Greenwich, Connecticut, features a painted chest set against a high wainscot with wallpaper above—an arrangement mirrored on the opposite wall.*

THIS PAGE AND OPPOSITE: *In the foyer of a new house in East Hampton, my client wanted the flavor of an old sea captain's residence, characterized by a few simple but strong objects. In a context of dark wood and white walls, I placed an oak entry table with a wave-form apron, a "tramp art" mirror found on a trip to France, and clean contemporary sconces.*

A combination of simple objects, artfully displayed in a foyer, tell a homeowner's story without a word having to be said.

THIS PAGE AND OPPOSITE: *In this playful Florida foyer for a color-loving client, I paired a Burmese console with a 1920s grotto chair; the family's Christmas cards, framed in black, hang above the stairs. The white walls and limestone floor serve as a good foil for the colorful artworks and rug. The outcome is low maintenance, especially for a Florida beach house, but does not look "practical."*

White walls, stone floors, and black iron stair railings leave a foyer open to interpretation and personal expression.

THIS PAGE: *A rustic country chair, well-chosen objects atop a chest, and a provocative photograph by Jack Spencer are all that is required in this stair hall.*
OPPOSITE: *This renovated 1920s house in Atlanta has a classic Southern foyer: The wide center hall has a white chair rail, with dark trim, that extends up the light-filled stairwell and a double door leading out to the backyard. The close architectural relationship between my client's trumeau mirror and the doorframe beside it was a happy accident.*

I love a wide central hallway with creaky floors and loads of natural light. This captures the essence of the South.

Living Rooms

ost of us feel kind of guilty that we do not use our living rooms all that often, but let's face it: The idea that you are going to use every square inch of your house every day is unrealistic. To me, rooms are like friends—they can't be everything to everybody all the time, and you just have to appreciate them for what they are capable of providing. It is OK for a space to be a little bit special and spared life's everyday wear and tear. That is what your living room is for—it exists to be beautiful, and rather than feeling guilty about not being in it all the time, have realistic expectations of its performance and enjoy it when the moment arrives to do so. You don't need to live in your living room. You just need to love it.

Because you are not in it all the time, you can make your living room into a real showplace, one that is innovative as well as inviting. It is more about beauty than practicality, less about function than what you are capable of imagining and expressing, so the living room is the place to push the envelope and design something not just dazzling and luxurious, but provocative and unexpected. It's the perfect place for all your investment pieces, too—the best art, objects, and furniture.

Even though you are not going to be in it every day, when your living room does get used, it has to hit its marks: The space can be a real showstopper in design terms and still fall flat if it is not set up properly. First and foremost: How many people does the room need to accommodate? If all the bedrooms in your house were full, would everyone have a place to sit down? How big is your extended family—if you had a big gathering and everyone showed up, could they all fit into your

PREVIOUS PAGES AND OPPOSITE: *The high-gloss green walls in this Manhattan living room were chosen to make the space feel inviting and comfortable no matter the season—cool in the hot months, warm and enveloping in winter. Though the rest of the palette is relatively subdued—ivory with notes of brown and paprika—gilt metal accents capture the light and give the quiet room a sprinkling of sparkle and glamour.*

living room comfortably and without disrupting the flow? Assess the size of your house—and think about who will be coming over—and scale the living room accordingly.

Once you have established the size, study the living room closely and determine its focal points. Is the entry door on axis with the fireplace? Is the wall on which you are going to set the sofa opposite a window? In my experience, a room usually has three good axes, and if you stand against each wall and look around, they reveal themselves quickly, enabling you to place furnishings harmoniously and maximize light and views.

Finding the living room's axes will also suggest how and where people will gather, allowing you to arrange the space for comfortable conversation—to select appropriate pieces for primary and secondary zones, those that will draw larger groupings, as well as the more intimate gatherings. Similarly, you will want bigger and smaller seating to accommodate different-size people, but to have it arranged so as to create harmony and balance at different scales and natural relationships between chair heights and the styles of arms and legs. Creative seating arrangements typically require that you "float" some furniture, and the floating pieces should look interesting and alluring from every angle—so that, simply by arranging the room, you have created something beautiful to look at.

Some useful rules can help you pull it all together. Make sure the rug fits the room: twelve inches from the walls, two inches from the hearth. Curtains should break like the cuffs on a pair of pants—not too short, as floors are invariably uneven, nor cascading into big puddles of fabric. Multiple light sources, evenly distributed around the room and all on dimmers, produce a flattering ambient glow while highlighting artworks, conversation areas, and accent points. Set your coffee table 14 inches (36cm) from the sofa. And above all, do not neglect the "fifth wall"—the ceiling: Just as you have introduced a mix of fabrics and textures into the upholstered pieces, treat the ceiling with a striking color, a lustrous lacquered finish, warm wood paneling, or a shimmering tea paper.

It sounds like a lot of effort for an occasional room, I know. But it's worth it, and you will know when you have it right: Everyone will be having a great time and telling you how beautiful it all looks, though they won't be able to say exactly why. The reason? It just works.

In a corner of the same space, a custom banquette facilitates a cozy dining area (all my rules about dining rooms go out the window in space-challenged New York apartments). The bold trellis pattern on all the Roman shades wraps the room with a play on geometry.

OPPOSITE AND THIS PAGE:
The word iridescent *comes to mind when I look at this double-height light-filled living room in Manhattan's West Village district. The subtle shimmer of Shawn Dulaney's painting perfectly captures the room's soft glow, and the surfaces of the Murano glass lamps add sparkle. I also love the profiles of the French armchairs, which I discovered in England.*

The most desirable and irreplaceable element in any room is the presence of natural light. It is simply magical.

The soft colors and air of tradition in this formal living room are counterbalanced by the colorful contemporary painting. The ten-foot-long custom sofa required two coffee tables—also custom, and finished in a lacquered linen with brass trim.

40

This view of a glamorous New York living room, on Fifth Avenue overlooking Central Park, features three standout elements: a brass and onyx coffee table by Philippe Hiquily, the Karel Appel painting, and the view. Accordingly, everything else, including the furnishings, rug, and curtains, is neutral-toned and discreet.

42

THIS PAGE AND OPPOSITE: *In the same room, a remarkable metal artwork by Roy Lichtenstein hangs above a 1940s Italian cabinet by one of my favorite designers from the period, Paolo Buffa. The art deco vases look just as good with or without flowers.*

THIS PAGE: *This living room overlooks beautiful gardens in a nature preserve. Blue and green faded floral print curtains line the room's perimeter, bringing the happy garden colors inside year-round.* OVERLEAF: *In this sunny Florida living room, gauzy pale gray sheer curtains capture sunlight and do not obscure the stunning views.*

46

This living room, in a 1920s house in Birmingham, mixes the antique and the modern and benefits from metallic elements—the gilt-framed mirror, the chunky brass lamps, and the profiles on the step-down coffee table arrangement.

THIS PAGE AND OPPOSITE: *The piece opposite the sofa is a bit of a hybrid—larger than a chaise, smaller than a sofa—but is perfectly scaled for the room. Two wing chairs by the windows flank a French gueridon table with a marble top. The accessories are simple, geometric, and in keeping with a living room that is masculine and tightly edited.*

THIS PAGE: *A pair of English hall chairs flanks a 1940s French cabinet topped with an arrangement of wooden jars; "insect artist" Christopher Marley created the framed displays of exotic butterflies.* OPPOSITE: *The painting, by Isabel Bigelow, was commissioned for the room and served as its decorative starting point. Like the artwork, the patterned rug is subtle but strong, and the high-gloss, highly reflective sage green ceiling seems to double the room in height.*

When a big statement piece takes command of the room, all of the other furnishings should quietly recede to restore balance.

A quartet of paintings by Wolf Kahn, in a living room in a historic Atlanta house, brightens this comfortably welcoming, neutral-toned Southern space. The printed linen on the chairs complements the gray, blue, and ivory color scheme.

Dining Rooms

I grew up in Florida, which I still call home most of the time. But as a child, I spent all of my holidays and summers on the Alabama farm where my grandparents lived. They were deep in the country, where lunch is called dinner and dinner is called supper, and as you can imagine, they took mealtime very seriously. Three times a day, a cloth went down on the long dining table; the serving bowls were filled with fresh foods freshly prepared and passed from hand to hand. Afterward everything was washed, dried, and put away in its proper place—only to be taken out again a few hours later so the ritual could be repeated.

Setting up and breaking down the table, preparing all that food, and spending time together really was a full-time occupation. I would wash the dishes for my grandmother and think, *My God, why are we doing this?* And now, don't you know, I cherish the memory of every last one of those dinners and suppers. When my grandmother died, I asked if I might have her serving bowls, in which I had passed around so many butter beans and lady peas. Whenever I take one of them in my hands, the aromas and flavors come flooding back, along with the sounds and images of family, of an idyllic time of life. And I am reminded, over and again, how important it is to sit down at table, to make it special, and to take that extra step.

That is why—even though, like the living room, it doesn't get used all the time—the dining room is a very important space. It is the ceremonial and emotional center of your

PREVIOUS: *For an Atlanta client with a love of sunny colors, I created a dining room with a yellow strié wallpaper and comparably colored curtains with a chevron pattern. Chairs covered in a blue Ottoman fabric surround an Italian table.* OPPOSITE: *This Charlotte, North Carolina, dining room is finished in neutral shades of taupe, which creates greater freedom to choose colorful flowers and table settings. The round table works well with the curved chair backs; the chandelier mixes rock and clear crystals with amethyst.*

house, the place where memories are made, at wedding and anniversary parties, holiday dinners, and other milestone occasions; where glasses are lifted amidst laughter and tears; and long hours are passed enjoying a great meal and each other's company. And also like the living room, the dining room needs to rise unfailingly to the moment: Without question, when you enjoy those special nights, the space itself needs to be as memorable as—and supportive of—the events that transpire within it.

You need to start with great acoustics—nothing ruins the mood of a festive dinner faster than the harsh echoes of raised voices. Think about upholstered walls, wallpaper, and, especially, wood paneling, which I love for its clubby, warm, and enveloping qualities. Curtains, too, are a must, as much for color and pattern as for their sound-absorptive properties. And though a lot of people worry about the mess, I am a great believer in a dining room rug. Just make sure it has got a pattern and can be cleaned up with relative ease, though no house has been properly christened until a glass of red wine has been sloshed onto a carpet. Do not get too plush a rug, however, or your guests won't be able to easily move their chairs.

Both lighting and color contribute strongly to warmth and drama. Having a palette of light sources—a chandelier or lantern, sconces or lamps, and picture lights, all of them on dimmers—enables you to more precisely fine-tune the mood as the evening goes from quiet to festive to contemplative. Your chandelier should be 66 to 69 inches (168 to 175 cm) off the floor, and if you have sconces above your sideboard, don't put lamps there as well. Deep colors, especially at night, give dining rooms richness, sex appeal, and a sense of occasion and typically prove flattering to the diners.

Comfortable dining chairs, of course, remain essential, and you will need to have at least eight of them. Never more than twelve, however, or your welcoming dining space will start to resemble a corporate conference room. I have to seat a total of eighteen when my own family gets together, so we drag in some extra chairs from other rooms—that way you don't lose the warmth or have empty seats when a gathering is smaller. Make sure you have at least 36 inches (91 cm) of space in which to pull back the chairs, and that your rug extends at least the same distance beyond the table.

This octagonal dining pavilion has views in all directions and invites the garden in. As the ceiling and room shape make the big statements here, I created a quiet interior with a seagrass rug and neutral-toned fabrics. The chairs, adorned with rows of buttons, surround a large round dining table.

To maintain a sense of intimacy no matter the number of guests, select a table that is adjustable in size, so that you can add or subtract leaves; I would recommend keeping the leaves in an easy place to access—for example, under the sofa if it is skirted—so you don't have to dig them out of the basement or the attic. Sideboards or chests will provide additional surfaces from which to serve and also enable you to store linens, candles, and tableware close to where they will be needed.

Once you have the major elements in place, do not neglect the tabletop: beautiful crystal and gleaming silver, but simple china—I think food looks best against a background of white or ivory. Having said that, I must admit that Southern women are china collectors, so I always encourage my clients to buy multiple sets and mix and match them, rather than using the same china every time—basically, you're building yourself a "wardrobe" of tabletop items. Everyone enjoys dining by candlelight, but be sure that tabletop illumination does not obscure your guests' views of one another. The same goes for floral arrangements: Use as many as you would like without crowding, but keep them low-rise and out of people's faces. Above all, avoid candles and flowers with fragrances—they will compete with, or even overwhelm, the food.

Take your time setting the table—make it into a ceremony that can be passed from one generation to the next. During the holiday season, I actually begin two days before Christmas Eve, layering the table as though it were a cake: first the thick felt I prefer as a liner; then my linen cloth, to give it time for the wrinkles to relax; then the plates, glasses, and hurricane candles; and, of course, the flowers, which have a day to open up and look so much prettier. Over time, my two girls—understanding the importance of the ritual—got involved and enjoyed and appreciated being included. When finally everyone pulls their knees up under the table, and all that fabulous food lands in front of them, it's truly a special moment, an experience that never loses its appeal.

You will know you have gotten it right if, once dinner is finished, your family and friends linger, sometimes for hours, reluctant to let the evening end. If they all jump up after the last bite of dessert and offer to do the dishes, it's not a good sign.

Jim designed this New York dining room for a client seeking the flavor of a private club, an effect achieved principally with this urbane and luxurious zebra wood paneling. A custom parchment cabinet, contemporary Murano glass lamps, and a deco Venetian mirror complete the room.

OPPOSITE AND THIS PAGE:
*Chairs upholstered in mohair
surround a dining table with
a hammered silver base and a
rosewood top. The wool
carpet and curtains contribute
warmth, while the silver-leaf
tea paper ceiling captures
the light, makes the low
ceiling seem higher, and lends
a glamour appropriate to a
Fifth Avenue apartment.
The painting, by Victor
Brauner, dates from 1942.*

Whether your dining room is intimate or grand,
don't overlook any surface. Walls, ceiling,
floor—each offers the chance to layer in details.

THIS PAGE AND OPPOSITE: *My husband, Jim, paneled this space, which gave definition to a large dining room that would have otherwise been an expanse of Sheetrock; the paneling also helped me to properly locate the mirror, artworks, and objects. The traditional mahogany furnishings contrast with the aqua strié wall color and more saturated tones of the curtains and chair fabric, enabling the room to be formal but not somber. The William Yeoward "Tatiana" hurricane candles are my all-time personal favorites.*

THIS PAGE AND OPPOSITE: *The neutral tones in this open, airy Florida beach house dining room serve as a simple canvas for colorful floral arrangements and tableware. The room's play on curves suggests a North African influence that is entirely appropriate to the climate and location.*

Pops of bright color in flowers or accessories keep a neutral-toned dining room lively no matter the season.

THIS PAGE AND OPPOSITE: *I wrapped the walls of this dining room, in a 1920s Georgian residence, in green wool, carrying the fabric into the curtains—the effect is quiet, enveloping, and very dramatic. The color also serves as an excellent backdrop for MaryBeth Thielhelm's stormy seascape. The midcentury Italian buffet, by Paolo Buffa, creates a moment of surprise in the traditional setting.*

PREVIOUS: *Gray silk wallpaper and a blue Tibetan rug set the tone in this Birmingham dining room. An English dumbwaiter, an Irish mirror, a contemporary brass pedestal, a midcentury rosewood Danish buffet, and a Chinese screen all complement, rather than contradict, one another.* ABOVE AND OPPOSITE: *To enliven this very traditional Richmond dining room, in which all of the furniture is English, I introduced a lighthearted damask wallpaper, contemporary artworks by Michael Abrams, and a pretty crystal chandelier.*

THIS PAGE AND OPPOSITE: *In this living/dining room in a Savannah loft, I unified the different zones with two-inch wood blinds and patterned curtains on all the windows, then differentiated between them by using contrasting rugs. The antique French farm table fits well with chairs covered in horsehair. The zinc billiards light dates from the 1920s.*

79

Kitchens

veryone has a memory of a favorite kitchen. Whether it was your own mom's kitchen or at a friend's or relative's house, there is surely an experience in your past that inspired you to create your own special kitchen.

Jim and I had been married for about six months when a kitchen directly changed the course of our lives. We had three children, two from Jim's first marriage and one from mine. Our plate was very full: Jim had just started his design firm, and I was busy managing our household and the children's schedules. We had not discussed having children of our own, as we were having a hard time even keeping up with what we already had. Funny how things can change so quickly depending on the course of a day.

Jim had an appointment with a family he was working for and was there for most of the day. Seeing how worn down he was in the afternoon, the client offered to make him a sandwich and they relocated to the kitchen, where she was cooking dinner for her family, five boys and a husband. Jim remembers the smells as mouthwatering, and he fell into a quick trance. He barely remembers the sandwich, but to this day he can recount in detail how the boys each arrived in the kitchen after school, grabbed a snack, greeted Jim, and moved on to their respective activities. It was a very busy scene, with the children and their friends coming and going, but the client graciously kept up with it all and at the same time made sure that Jim was being properly looked after. Her husband finally came home and was promptly served a cocktail. Jim knew it was dinnertime, so he said good-bye and left.

PREVIOUS: *One of my favorite things in a kitchen is a banquette. This one, in a corner at once cozy and sunny, is paired with a Saarinen table and durable bistro chairs and upholstered in an easy-to-clean fabric.* OPPOSITE: *My client renovated this kitchen himself and did a good job: I like the seamless marble countertop and backsplash, sconces flanking the sink, and soft Roman shades.*

This kitchen was too small to accommodate a conventional island but too large not to have something at its center. My client's solution was this table, which combines aesthetic appeal with a hardworking surface and useful storage and drawer space. The glass-front upper cabinets, icebox latches, and bin pulls on the drawers are all appropriate for a house built in the 1920s.

Jim came home, walked into our kitchen, and said, "I want us to have a child together." We had our girl around a year later. Her name is Nellie Jane, and she is now twenty-six years old. She was the puzzle piece we were missing in our family and to this day is the glue that holds everyone together. I often wonder what would have happened if Jim had gone to another house that day!

As any realtor will tell you, a good kitchen can really add value to your house. But as this story makes clear, a good kitchen's true value can be measured by the quality it brings to your life. As a Southerner, I know one essential truth: Cooking is powerful. My family and I have prepared and shared countless meals together, and the quickest way I know to bring everyone together happily and harmoniously is to prepare something delicious and ring the dinner bell. That is why a well-functioning kitchen remains so important. And creating one is fairly simple: The basic rule is that the person who makes the meals should be satisfied with the layout. Everyone will reap the rewards of the cook's pleasure, so make sure she or he has plenty of input into the design process.

Start with the layout and interior organization rather than the decoration—while your living room can exist for the sole purpose of looking beautiful, your kitchen cannot: It needs to function properly first, and look good second. My favorite layout is U-shaped, with the cooktop and range hood as the focal point, the sink directly opposite them in the kitchen island, and counters and cabinets wrapping the sides. This arrangement gives you plenty of room in which to maneuver and also provides an abundance of useful counter space (of which you can never have too much). As well, positioning the sink and dishwasher in the island enables the cook to talk to others while prepping food or cleaning up.

Storage is just as important in a kitchen as elsewhere in a house, but it demands a bit more forethought and nuance. For example, I prefer floor-to-ceiling cabinets to big walk-in pantries, as they let you see everything at a glance. Also important is the depth of your upper cabinets—a minimum of 12 inches (30 cm) lets you accommodate your oversize dinner plates and chargers. In the same way that a smart closet designer can maximize the efficiency of a tight space, I like to design kitchen drawers with custom dividers that enable you to organize your utensils based on what you need and the frequency with which you use them. If you have the space,

In my own kitchen, durable leather barstools that swivel pull
up to a large island beneath painted industrial pendants.

When I look at a kitchen, I do not see cabinets, counters, or appliances. I smell food. I hear the wonderful noises of everyday life. I see kitchens that fill with people, and then empty out, over and over again. I see kitchens that are full of life.

you can even put in a silver cloth–lined, locking drawer for your sterling—which means you will occasionally use your best flatware for everyday occasions, a good habit to form. And be sure the dishwasher is near the silverware drawer and the cabinets for glasses and dishes: You don't want to take more than two steps to put everything away.

The more efficient the layout, the easier things will flow, and the more you will actually enjoy using your kitchen. The sink, for example, should be flanked by the dishwasher and the trash, so you can load the former quickly and easily, and pull out the latter to sweep your cuttings into it. Flow and efficiency are closely related to major appliances, both the old-fashioned kind and new ones coming onto the market. It used to be that you had a big refrigerator/freezer in one place and a dishwasher in another, and you were basically a slave to their sizes and locations. But the multiple variations on these machines that are now available have completely changed the landscape of the traditional kitchen. Most of us are used to the independent cooktop and separate wall-mounted double ovens. But are you familiar with the small "dishwasher drawer" set into the kitchen island beside the sink? It lets you do a small load easily and economically, as you don't have to run the big one for just a couple of pots and plates. Similarly, you can incorporate refrigerator and freezer drawers into the island or counters—these options augment, rather than replace, traditional appliances, and provide you with more options and greater flexibility.

The cooking area offers another opportunity to maximize convenience and flow. Position your spices, utensils, and pots and pans within arm's length of your cooktop, and try to have at least 2 feet (0.6 m) of counter space to both the right and left of it (the same goes for the sink). A minimum of 18 inches (46 cm) next to your oven will give you room to set down something that is hot. Never install a microwave higher than 4 feet (1.2 m), or you will have a hazard on your hands. And keep in mind the noise level in your kitchen, which can be dismayingly high. Apart from using sound-absorptive materials wherever possible, install a remote or in-line exhaust fan to minimize the noise from your range hood.

I also believe in building in as many things as possible—a designated coffee station, for example, with its own purified water supply, set into a cabinet with coffee, filter, and sugar storage, the whole thing lined with easy-to-clean stainless steel. Under-the-counter wine coolers—for red and white, set at different temperatures—are great, as is, in a different way, a dog food station at the end of your kitchen island: a pull-out cabinet you can fill from the top, and a chute at the bottom with the bowl tucked away beneath it.

The lighting in a kitchen is critical. I rely on three types: recessed downlighting set halfway between the island and counters, the cans set at intervals of about 4 feet (1.2 m); pendants above the island; and under-the-cabinet lights. All of them on dimmers: No one wants to be blinded when they come down for a cup of coffee at five A.M.

The eat-in kitchen serves as a second or backup family room, so it is nice to have as many dining options as possible—an old-fashioned table and chairs as well as barstools along an island, to cite a popular combination. If you have the room to add a wood extension to the island, so that it feels more like a dedicated dining area, so much the better. When it comes to chairs and barstools, don't be impractical. Artificial leather or washable soft suede are both stain-resistant and can be wiped clean with a damp sponge. If you have kids, make sure you make it easier on yourself by choosing cleanable materials for all kitchen seating—otherwise you are just setting yourself up for failure.

Finally—and I say this all the time—be realistic about your lifestyle. When selecting materials, make choices that have the durability to match your temperament. I love honed white marble countertops, but if stains and scratches will bother you, choose something, such as Silestone, that is a tougher material. Do not set your kitchen up for parties and entertaining if what you like to have are intimate evenings with family and friends. A kitchen is a place for honesty and a true assessment of how you live and what your real needs are.

OPPOSITE: *A Caio Fonseca painting brightens this casual country breakfast room, in which rush chairs surround a simple painted farm table.* THIS PAGE: *This kitchen overlooks a golf course, and so I made the view the focal point. Light wood floors, white surfaces, and wicker shades and stools keep things clean and simple.*

Simple clean surfaces and natural woven textures, especially wicker and straw—in any kind of kitchen, the combination always says *relax*.

THIS PAGE AND OPPOSITE: *The previous owners of this Richmond, Virginia, residence had installed the turquoise glass tiles in the kitchen backsplash—a decision that inspired my decorative choices throughout the house. The color found its way into the chair fabric in the adjoining breakfast room and, quite dramatically, in the unusual "glass bottle" chandelier. It serves as a good lesson: If something works, do not hesitate to use it—even if it wasn't your own idea.*

THIS PAGE: *This large square table with eight chairs— two per side—represents one of my favorite combinations. It's more unexpected, in a breakfast room, than a round table.* OPPOSITE: *To display my client's collection of blue-and-white porcelain, I chose a tall black cabinet with a woven-wire front. Black "bamboo" chairs surround the informal chestnut dining table.*

In a breakfast room designed for casual dining, the experience should be made up of equal parts style, comfort, and practicality.

Believe it or not, my design for this big Nashville kitchen began with my desire to use white porcelain knobs on the cabinets. That led to the white marble countertop and backsplash, the milk glass schoolhouse pendant lamps, and, by way of contrast, the green-painted island and cabinetry (the boards above and around the doorways are a half-shade lighter). This is a real working kitchen, with two sinks and dishwashers tucked into the island, and it represents my own ideal layout.

This breakfast room looks out onto a busy street, and though I didn't want to lose the sunlight, some view management was in order—thus the sheer café curtains on the lower windows. I surrounded the French marble-topped table, with its robust iron base, with oversize wicker chairs, and set the arrangement atop an antique Oushak rug.

99

THIS PAGE AND OPPOSITE: *My client inherited this modern kitchen from the previous owners. The breakfast area represents a singular study in contrast: Vintage midcentury George Nakashima chairs and a pair of classic Saarinen tables sit beneath John Mitchell's 1755 twenty-four-segment engraving of "the British and French dominions" in North America—the most important map in my client's collection.*

THIS PAGE: *Jim designed this Jacksonville kitchen, which combines simple country wood cabinets lightly washed with white paint and beautifully figured slabs of marble on the island, countertops, and backsplash. Our client requested unusual lighting in every room; this is a vintage chandelier that we found in Los Angeles.* OPPOSITE: *This simple setting in the breakfast room corner gets a bit of swing from the crescent-moon chair backs and curving table legs.*

THIS PAGE AND OPPOSITE: *In this big kitchen/dining/family room that Jim and I developed for a young family, the soft and pretty fern pattern on the wallpaper continues onto the curtains and Roman shades. The built-in banquette in the window, four club chairs, and barstools offer a number of ways in which to enjoy the room.*

The two seemingly antique armoires on the left are in fact custom-made floor-to-ceiling pantries. Sheer curtains in the glass-front upper cabinets conceal glasses and dishes. The four chairs, upholstered in a durable, comfortable fabric, surround an ottoman, the top of which can be removed to store blankets and throws.

THIS PAGE: *The architect, Bill Beeton, chose to run the shelves in an adjoining hallway bar in front of the window—it suggests an earlier life for the new house and adds to the easygoing atmosphere.*
OPPOSITE: *In this country-style kitchen in East Hampton, simplicity in all things: the butcher block island top, burlap shades on the hanging fixture, a range hood finished in bead board, and bamboo shades. I found the spongeware pitchers for the shelves on the island.*

If you do not use it for daily functional purposes, open shelving in a kitchen is an excellent way to display collections.

I placed distinctive reproduction Orkney chairs at either end of this sawhorse table, which stands atop a blue dhurrie flat-weave rug. The lively print on the curtains and Roman shades stands in counterpoint to the more discreetly patterned upholstered chairs.

110

OPPOSITE: *Jim designed this narrow galley kitchen in a New York apartment and chose mahogany millwork to serve as a dark frame for the richly patterned canvas of the marble backsplash. Beneath the marble countertop on the island, we installed leather panels with metal studs.*

THIS PAGE: *A ribbon of onyx, between two levels of mahogany cabinetry, really makes a statement in this Florida butler's pantry, which has the flavor of a train car.*

Polished mahogany cabinets set the stage for sophisticated grown-up entertaining—and can be as stunning as they are functional.

Family Rooms

PREVIOUS AND OPPOSITE: *Arranging this double-height family room was complicated by its narrow dimensions and the presence of the stairway. Ultimately we chose to make a virtue of the liability and set the major furniture pieces against the stairway. The midcentury-inspired armchairs pair well with the milk chocolate backgrounds in the bookcases; the color creates depth and helps the objects to stand out. My design for the feet-friendly leather coffee table includes a removable tray.*

116

*I*f the living and dining rooms are reserved for special occasions and carefully crafted to achieve very specific kinds of effects, the family room is precisely the opposite. We are in there constantly—feet up and relaxing, reading or watching TV, surrounded by kids and pets, enjoying the cozy, comfortable atmosphere and not worrying about spilling on the rug or breaking something. In the family room, beauty plays second fiddle to practicality—if I had to choose one word to describe it, I would pick *durable*.

And yet you cannot just let your family room turn into a free-for-all. In my experience, a successful space derives from a sound plan rather than from the items you put into it, and that is especially the case with a room that takes a daily, nearly nonstop beating. Think about your kitchen: No room works harder, but because it is well organized and there is a place for everything, you can easily restore it to order, even after you have cooked a large meal. The family room is the kitchen in which you live. If you have a system that lets you put everything away, it will look presentable—and even pretty—and still be as user-friendly and welcoming as you would like it to be.

Certain architectural considerations come into play, notably the family room's proximity to the kitchen—ideally the two are adjacent, as food should be quickly and easily accessible. The family room is also a great place for beams and wood paneling, both of which convey a sense of coziness and intimacy; in cold climates, heated stone floors can be especially comfortable. I find that bookcases lend a great deal of character—but you have to put books in them, in addition to the personal objects and snapshots that consume shelf space in a room meant for parents and children to share.

For this high-ceilinged family room in a new East Hampton home, which enjoys abundant sunlight, my clients requested a blue and white scheme. I wanted to ring a change on this traditional combination, and so upholstered the major sofas and chairs in turquoise, mixed that color with indigo in the patterned fabrics, and chose a predominantly indigo rug. The white-painted coffee table is vintage Baker.

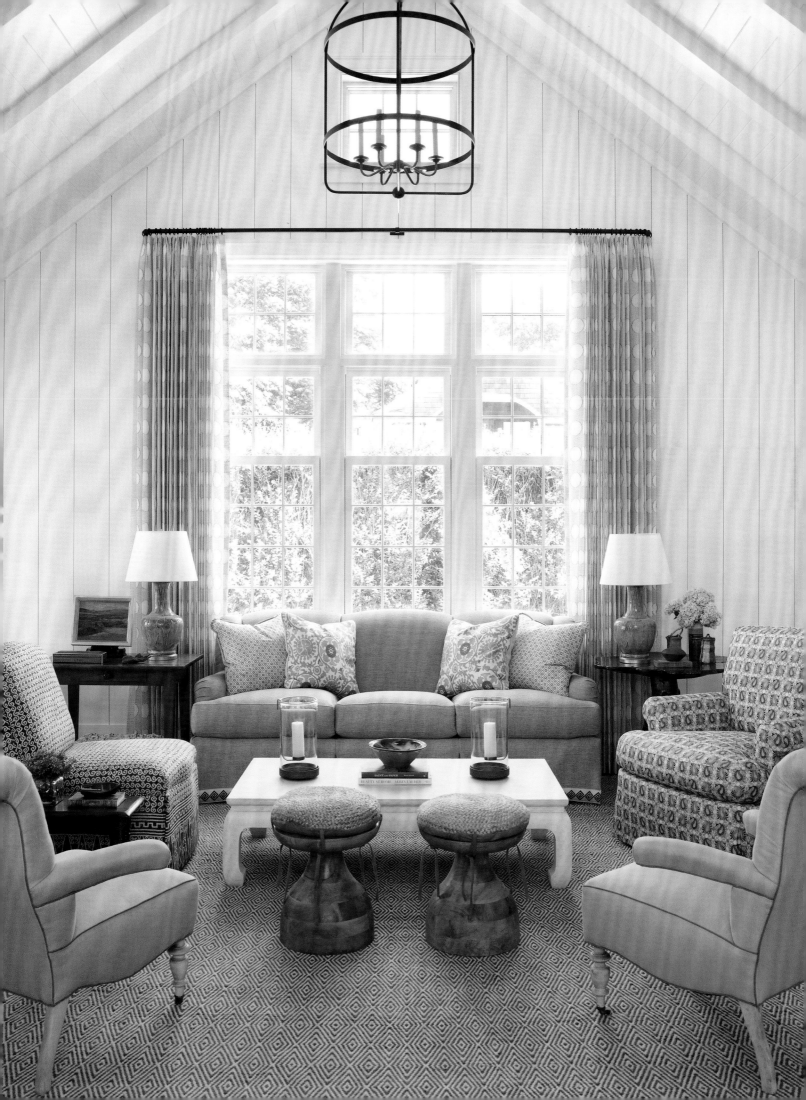

On the opposite side of the same blue and white room, the two diminutive English armchairs were selected for their high comfort quotient and unusual profiles. Patterned sheer curtains cover the windows, and I chose unusual tables, including the tree-stump drink table and a Moroccan coffee table inlaid with elephant figures. The box beneath it is covered in seashells.

120

Furniture should be all about comfort and indestructibility. I am convinced that the key to every man's happiness lies in his ability to put his feet up, so have plenty of ottomans, a coffee table you can reach with your legs, and a sofa that is long enough for the biggest person in your house to stretch out on, with low arms and overstuffed pillows (sit on upholstered pieces before purchasing them if you can). An extra layer of comfort comes from motion, so think about chairs that swivel, recline, and rock; unlike the living room, in which furniture groupings tend to be widely spaced, the family room can be more closely arranged and even a bit crowded. Above all, fabrics and carpets need to be rugged, stain-resistant, and, if possible, washable.

Two things that often get overlooked in family room design are light control and its close cousin, privacy. I typically specify layers of window treatments, for example solar shades and curtains, for different times: the former to keep the sun glare off the TV by day, the latter to deliver a complete blackout by night and protect your windows from the curious eyes of neighbors or passersby.

And speaking of the all-important television: Make sure it is set at the right angle, so that you do not strain your neck. One needs to be especially careful if the screen is mounted above a fireplace, as the closer you get, the more extreme the tilt of your head. I find as well that it is aesthetically very effective to cut out a niche for the set, so that it's flush with the wall rather than projecting outward from it. It is only a difference of inches, but the screen becomes a much less intrusive presence in the room. Failing that, some sort of detailing—even if it is only a frame—can make a TV seem less like technology and more like a design object. Most decorators have now accepted, and even embraced, wall-mounted TVs—they are here to stay.

Finally, a woodburning fireplace in a family room is a must for me, both functionally and aesthetically. Nothing is more fundamentally reassuring than a fire, and even though we live in Florida, when the temperature dips we grab every available chance to enjoy one.

In the living room of this sunny oceanfront house, the faded blues and greens reflect the tropical landscape and the water just beyond the window. Because the colors are light, the fabrics and rug are stain-resistant.

I hated to part with the "peace sign" flag, which was made around the time of the Woodstock music festival in upstate New York and is a splendid example of modern-era folk art, but it was perfect for this Savannah loft, so I gave in. The room is zoned into discrete areas—a midcentury partners desk by the window, a pair of Italian armchairs by the fireplace, and a principal sitting space with a pair of barrel-backed leather chairs—and can be enjoyed in multiple ways by gatherings of all sizes.

124

THIS PAGE: *This double-height, handsomely paneled family room had windows set at varying heights, and I decided to embrace the difference and hang the curtains accordingly. My client had traditional taste in furniture but adventurous taste in art, and so the furniture, decor, and seagrass rug collectively serve as a quiet counterpoint to the bold canvas by Terry Weiss above the sofa.*
OVERLEAF: *In fall and winter, hunters with their dogs tromp through in muddy boots, so all of the fabrics are durable and easy to clean—you can grab a glass of whiskey and fearlessly put your feet up.*

Another collaboration between my husband, Jim, and myself, this family room received oak paneling with a lime wash, on which we hung the house's eight original architectural drawings (dating from the 1920s). The big leather ottoman/coffee table was designed to accommodate the family's desire to put their feet up.

The soft colors and tranquil atmosphere in this space belie the fact that my clients have three little girls. But family rooms do not have to be dark if you make appropriate fabric choices. I designed the large ottoman to include drawers on both sides, which hold extra pillows and throws. An antique writing box on a stand serves as a side table.

My clients love deep, saturated color, and though it is not visible in the photograph, this room took its cues from an amethyst chandelier. The aubergine velvet sofa came next, followed by the velvet cut stripe on the club chairs, and we were fortunate to find a rug that tied it all together. The oak walls with linen panels contribute to the room's deep sense of quiet and warmth.

PREVIOUS: *For this high-ceilinged room in Nashville, with transom windows above the beams, I chose a feminine color palette to contrast with the more masculine flavor of the rustic wood over the fireplace and herringbone-pattern wood doors. Seagrass rugs define two seating areas separated by a console table. The painting is by Shawn Dulaney.* OPPOSITE: *For a Connecticut family with three children, I fashioned a warm and comfortable, neutral-toned family room in which to watch TV and enjoy a fire, enlivened by a vintage olive wood coffee table.*

138

This family room, in a Florida beach house, was designed to be used by teenagers, evidenced by the sectional, which can be separated to form a pair of twin beds. The unlined matchstick blinds and wicker-sided club chairs pair well with the wicker mirrors—which I found at the Paris flea market— over the French console table.

My husband, Jim, figured out all the angles in this paneled attic pool room in Jacksonville, a complicated puzzle that works perfectly. My client wanted a very specific type of felt for the tabletop—which fortunately was available in the perfect shade of red, echoed in the chair fabric and Roman shade. A TV and bar, complete with wine cooler, make this the perfect man's getaway.

Libraries

ot all of my clients ask for libraries, but the ones who do understand their value. They are about reading, of course, but in a larger sense, the function of a library is to inspire creativity, in whatever artistic medium captivates you: writing, drawing, even sewing. Maybe you retire to your library to think about your work, pay bills, or sit with your laptop. A serene, contemplative space in which the creativity that surrounds you on the shelves can somehow seep into your own mind and set fire to your imagination is a place from which any house can benefit.

That said, a library is first and foremost a place for books—storing, collecting, displaying, accessing, and cherishing them. Some people have books that are purely decorative, that they have gathered together in large measure for their beauty, color, and texture. I understand that, but I am more in favor of having books you'd actually want to read and revisit, a living library as opposed to one that is inert. Decide how you want to arrange your books. Alphabetically? By subject or color? Fiction versus nonfiction? Do you want the large-format illustrated books in a separate case or stacked on tables? A special shelf for your favorites? This kind of thoughtful engagement with books only increases your appreciation of what they have to offer and how important they are to the life of the mind.

PREVIOUS: *A Robert Motherwell print brings a jolt of color and life to this traditional space.* OPPOSITE: *The light cerused oak paneling and textured Roman shades and rug make this library feel warm and inviting and not in the least stuffy.*

I have said it before and I will say it again: Do not build bookshelves unless you have or want to have books. They add life to a room in ways that other objects simply cannot.

Bookcases should be adequate to your present and foreseeable needs and well designed—their animation comes from the volumes they contain. Handsomely finished wood looks great, but so does a deep lacquered color. The right shade, subdued yet rich, will give your library a greater sense of depth and foreground your collection more dramatically.

Personally, I like a library that is masculine and dark, and slightly underfurnished, with a few well-chosen pieces, antiques if possible—think about comfortable leather chairs, an upholstered sofa, or a partners desk, all of it atop a beautiful, slightly exotic carpet. In fact, the size of your library will suggest its use, and that use will dictate what you put in it—for example, a billiards or game table or a cabinet fitted with a bar.

However the library ultimately functions, good lighting is essential, especially as it is a space that—unlike the rest of your home—doesn't need a lot of natural light; atmospheric coziness adds to the contemplative mood. Your bookcases should be well enough lit for you to be able to read the titles on the spines; reading lamps need to be plentiful and properly positioned; overhead ambient lighting does not have to be overly brilliant but should create pools of illumination where they are needed; and, of course, all artworks should be properly lit.

A last thought: If possible, position your library in the quietest part of your house and insulate the walls. It is the perfect room in which to savor the beauty of silence.

I think it is absolutely essential to have a low drink table next to a club chair, and this traditional oak example makes an excellent casual complement to the English-style cantilever armchair (designed by my husband, Jim).

OPPOSITE: *This room was designed entirely around the beautiful landscape painting by Clay Wagstaff, which brings light and life into a darker space.*
THIS PAGE: *Two Chinese chairs flank an English oak mule chest. The pottery lamps, by Charlie West, contribute to the differing yet complementary styles of this vignette.*

THIS PAGE: *A map showing views of Savannah from 1891 is hung above a seating area in a master bedroom and has a quiet, commanding presence.* OPPOSITE: *Two extraordinary examples of celestial cartography by the seventeenth-century mathematician and cosmographer Andreas Cellarius, from my client's map collection, command this cozy corner—contrasting effectively with the simple contemporary desk, midcentury lamps, and industrial metal chair.*

I have always been fascinated by maps.
Not only are they an education, they also inspire
wanderlust and dreams of exploration.

Balancing elements on a library's bookshelves can be hard to get right, but it is made easier when you bring in things that you love and that reflect your personality. The room contains a lively mix of elements—the midcentury table and chair, a brown cowhide rug on the original heart pine floor, another classic from my client's map portfolio, and several pieces from a miniature car collection.

154

THIS PAGE AND OPPOSITE: *In this library and working office, in a very traditional house with twelve-foot-high ceilings, I installed bookcases on three walls and glazed the surfaces in a gray-blue finish. I emphasized the room's height with Roman shades and a bronze chandelier and introduced a European flavor with a mix of English and French antiques.*

PREVIOUS: *Leather books, bamboo blinds, and plush upholstery introduce warmth and comfort into this Connecticut library, which takes its colors from the hillside views.* ABOVE: *The stars on this remarkable antique flag reflect its maker's view of the states: The orderly rows above signify the North, while the rowdy irregular ones below stand for the South.* OPPOSITE: *Beneath a 1970s Murano chandelier, pie-shaped chairs surround a game table in a library lacquered a high-gloss Prussian blue.*

OPPOSITE AND THIS PAGE: *For a stylish, well-tailored client, I designed a complementary library, with a relaxing daybed nestled between a pair of leather trunks, a midcentury desk and chairs, and an alabaster chandelier. The warm and textured brown grass cloth wall covering and seagrass rug make the room as warm and enveloping as it is urbane.*

163

THIS PAGE AND OPPOSITE: *My client's Joan Miró artwork provided the opportunity to hang a picture on a bookcase, which adds an interesting layer to the experience and creates a focal point (I love that it's directly above the children's Lego sculptures, too). The glass coffee table inspired me to introduce a boldly patterned custom carpet.*

Vary the size and height of the bookshelves to suit your collections. A painting, hung on a busy bookcase, will establish a focal point.

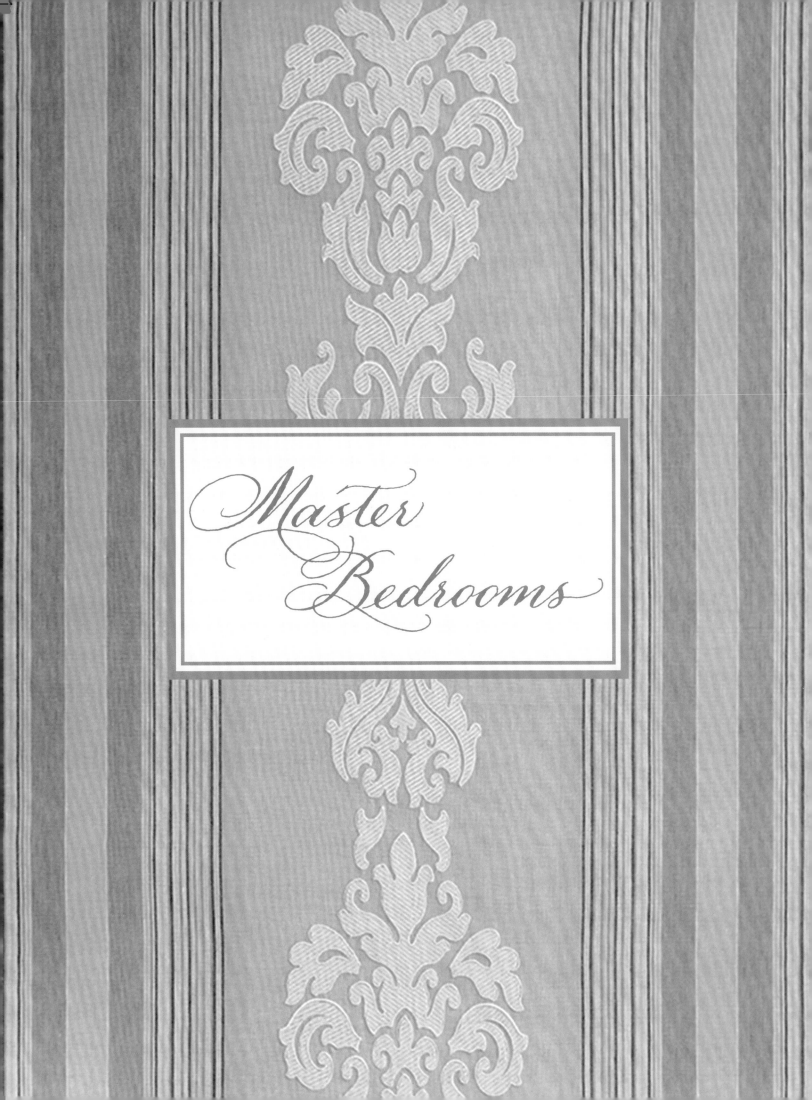

Master
Bedrooms

*I*n the narrative of the house, the master bedroom—in which you spend a third of your life—is a couple's sanctuary, the serene cocoon in which two people can enclose themselves and enjoy an intimate experience that is just about them. And because it is not a communal space, it can address the needs of a couple in a way that is highly specific and personal, enabling both individuals to emerge every day feeling rested, rejuvenated, and ready to take on the world. Since your bedroom is the first thing you see when you open your eyes in the morning, you need to give it the importance it deserves. I am all about soft bedrooms—my natural inclination is to create a soothing space layered with enveloping fabrics on the furnishings, windows, and floor. But it doesn't have to be that way. If your preference is for something bright and visually stimulating, by all means, go for it. The important thing is to design a room that speaks to you on a deep, and deeply gratifying, level.

I think the woman should take the design lead in the bedroom, and for several reasons. If she wakes up in a room that flatters her, it sets her at ease, and that is a win for the whole household—if she's happy, everybody is going to be happy. It is also the case that, if you decorate a bedroom around a woman, the man will fit into the scheme just fine, but the opposite is not typically the case: Men appreciate feminine bedrooms because they are attracted to women, but if the space looks like a bachelor pad, she will feel uncomfortable and excluded. In my experience, letting the woman be the room's inspiration has always proven to be a winning formula.

PREVIOUS: *Artworks constructed from embossed paper found at the Paris flea market add texture and shape to a gentle-hued bedroom in the Hamptons. I love the integrity of the 1940s Italian writing table's simple clean lines; its placement beside the bed offers different options for use.* OPPOSITE: *The custom-designed-and-built canopy bed echoes the room's tray ceiling.*

The bed panels are made from
a beautifully embroidered linen,
with the inside finished in an
ivory linen. The upholstered
headboard and pick-stitch quilt at
the bed's foot, in quiet shades of
blue-green, contribute to the
enveloping layers of softness. The
painting is by Clay Wagstaff.

170

Creating a bedroom in which a woman looks her best can be as simple as looking at the clothes she wears, as most of us know what colors suit us best. It's not foolproof, of course, but when designing a flattering bedroom, a peek at a woman's coloring serves as an excellent starting point.

It is nice, if you have the space, to create an anteroom or vestibule that serves as a buffer between the master suite and a home's public areas. Once you pass through it, the first thing you see, and the most beautiful element in the room, should be the bed. But the experience of the bed is no less important than its appearance, and a number of considerations go into perfecting it. It begins with a mattress precisely tuned to your ideal of comfort, fitted with the finest bed linens you can afford; it should be roughly 30 inches (76 cm) high and finished with a custom dust ruffle and two or three Euro shams, depending upon the size of the bed. Not too many pillows, however—if they are sticking out three feet from the headboard, you've gone too far.

Good reading lights are a must. I like the ones that attach to the headboard—the kind you see in hotels—and lamps on night tables must be at the right height to keep direct light from hitting you in the eyes. I would also recommend night tables with drawers, so you can easily sweep all the stuff that accumulates there out of sight. And I confess to a fondness for canopy beds, which offer a great opportunity for drama or to do something over the top. Plus, they are cozy: A canopy bed is a room within a room.

Don't forget the practicalities—flip the mattress four times a year, change your pillows annually, iron the sheets. And I always advise people to get a king-size bed, even if it is a tight fit within the room. Ultimately, the point of the room is to provide a good night's sleep—and as every married couple eventually discovers, the day you switch to a king bed is a happy one.

Once the bed has been perfected, a few simple gestures will dramatically enhance the experience: a comfortable rug underfoot and something pretty on the ceiling, even if it is just a color. Curtains add a layer of softness and mute sound, and I like to pair them with blackout shades, which deliver the perfect darkness that promotes sleep. A seating area, simply furnished, in which you can enjoy a glass of wine or a book, is a special treat. Make sure you have drink tables, ottomans, and floor lamps, to encourage relaxation and comfort.

My husband, Jim, developed the wood design for the shaped ceiling, which gives the space a sense of directionality and light (despite the single window). The pale green glass chandelier and similarly shaded upholstery, mirrored surfaces, and ivory-painted furniture give the bedroom unexpected glamour.

This monochrome bedroom is simplicity itself, finished almost entirely in soft shades of ivory and white. The custom-built canopy bed, with its pineapple finials, is enclosed by sheer unlined linen panels and features an embroidered top. A pair of projecting closets creates a niche for a love seat. The flower photo completes the serene setting.

In this master suite, in shades of lavender and gray, the king-size bed is flanked by a pair of mismatched but related large antique chests. I carried the valance fabric into the curtains, but restricted it to the leading edges, which delivers impact and interest and saves on expense. A wing chair designed by Bunny Williams adds a nice touch of comfort and style to this very soft, very Southern bedroom.

Being afraid of light colors in a bedroom
is like worrying about wearing
white jeans in summer—get over it!

PREVIOUS: *I found the queen-size four-poster bed for this Savannah loft bedroom and enlarged it into a king, adding the top, with its crown molding—an example of how an existing element can be customized and made more modern. The strongly graphic painted floor, by Savannah artist Bob Christian (who also color-washed the walls), plays well with the satin curtains and serves as a great alternative to a rug.* OPPOSITE AND THIS PAGE: *I chose an English leaf-pattern wallpaper and matching curtain fabric to wrap this space in a vibrant, happy green, a color that works well year-round in a bedroom. The suite was so large that I was able to place sitting areas at the foot of the bed and in an adjoining room, which is hung with family photos.*

My ultimate goal is not to successfully interpret my clients' desires—it is to create rooms that make them feel good about themselves.

THIS PAGE AND OPPOSITE: *I extended the posts on this eighteenth-century bed, adding panels made from silk with mohair appliqué embroidery and a starburst rosette on the ceiling. The silk velvet curtains with glass bead trim are good companions to the custom hand-painted Gracie mural paper featuring a selection of Georgia birds.*

184

For what I describe as a very happy feminine bedroom, for a client who loves pattern and color, I selected a lively wallpaper and carried it into the Roman shades. Other patterns continue on the embroidered bed hangings (with solid insides), bed pillows, an eighteenth-century botanical print, and the carpet. Glazed ceramic lamps flank the bed.

On the bedroom's French doors, I hung a solid ivory fabric with the patterned accents on the bottom and leading edge. The dominant fabric appears again on the club chairs in the room's sitting area, and I positioned a painting of a pastoral scene above the dresser. There is a lot that meets the eye in this suite, but the outcome is cheerful and welcoming rather than busy.

189

OPPOSITE AND THIS PAGE:
I designed the spool bed for this Hamptons house to work in harmony with the wood ceiling, adding simple white Roman shades and a pair of folk art paintings. A Venetian grotto shell mirror hangs above a 1940s French cabinet finished in parchment. The chair, also French, is covered in a linen stripe.

I confess: Light blue is my all-time favorite color for a master bedroom. I never tire of the peace and serenity it offers.

OPPOSITE AND THIS PAGE:
To neutralize the noise factor in this New York City bedroom, I introduced upholstered walls, an expansive rug, and heavy curtains. The bed features a chic shagreen headboard, and the pattern in the carpet echoes the columned legs of the deco chair. The painting, which I admired for its energy, is by Tad Wiley.

Create a cocoon with upholstered walls, thick curtains, and a plush rug, and all the world's noise and chaos will disappear.

Guest Rooms

*W*hat was the best experience you ever had in a five-star hotel? No doubt your room was beautifully decorated, and I am sure it was big and luxurious, the bath products were great, and the sheets were soft and perfectly pressed. But I will bet there were three things that made it especially memorable and distinct: Everything worked, you didn't need an engineering degree to operate the lights or the entertainment system, and, critically, nothing had been overlooked. The true definition of luxury, in my view, is thoughtfulness: the extent to which a hotel's management has anticipated your needs, considered how you might use the room, and arranged its elements accordingly. That level of care and concern, and the sense of absolute comfort and satisfaction it produced, is what made that hotel room stand out—and is precisely what you owe your houseguests.

I can't count the number of bad guest rooms I have seen—where the closets were stuffed with out-of-season clothes, the batteries in the TV remote were dead, and there were no window treatments—and I would never want my friends or family subjected to that, especially after they have traveled to see me. While you would like your guests to participate fully in the life of the house, you also want them to be able to withdraw when necessary, and with nothing missing from their experience, for your sake as well as theirs. Five-star thoughtfulness is the key to success.

PREVIOUS: *In this guest room, the weave of the African baskets plays off the texture of the grass cloth walls and wall-to-wall seagrass on the floor. The patchwork Oushak rug and ikat fabric on the headboards contribute to the global flavor.* OPPOSITE: *This perfectly neutral, unisex guest room includes all of the amenities and no extraneous decoration. The artwork was a gift to my clients from Atlanta artist Todd Murphy.*

Even the smallest, most simple guest room can feel luxurious and spacious—if the details have been carefully considered, and the gestures are welcoming and thoughtful.

Decoratively, guest rooms should be neither masculine nor feminine: beautiful but simple, and pleasing in color. I also do not believe that you should have too many personal touches in a guest room, such as monograms, family photos, or memorabilia—make it feel specially furnished for the guest, rather than the occupants of the house. Ample bedside tables with good reading lights, curtains and blackout shades, and a soft rug; a king-size bed if possible, with a good mattress and at least four pillows; and a comfortable reading chair will nicely complete the space. The secret to success lies in what a concierge might describe as the amenities: beside the bed or chair, books and current magazines; on the dresser, water and glasses on a tray, fruit and snacks in a basket, a good coffeemaker, and a vase of fresh flowers; desktop plugs, an iPod docking station or Bose stereo, a television, and an alarm clock; closets with plenty of hangers, extra blankets and pillows, and a luggage rack. Be sure to carefully stock the bath with all the things they might have forgotten, like shampoo, toothpaste, a razor, or sunscreen. And don't forget the blow-dryer—no one wants to pack one.

Get all of this right, and your guests will never forget how well looked after—and appreciated—you made them feel.

The white quilt, flower-print pillows, and framed flags set
the tone for this all-American, old-fashioned guest room.
Blinds and curtains provide extra privacy and lighting options.

This guest room was large enough for me to treat it like a luxury hotel suite. The two queen-size four-posters create coziness within the high-ceilinged space, and, though it is meant to be shared, the rectilinear bed enclosures suggest rooms within rooms. Whenever possible, I include benches at the foot of beds—they are great for unpacking suitcases.

The walls, chair, curtains, and even the lampshade in this tiny room are covered in brown-striped ticking, and everything is banded or trimmed in lipstick red. It is all very subtle—except for the not-so-subtle red ceiling that tops it all off. The shield-shaped mirror hanging before the windows provides a focal point and gives the cozy space a bit of an edge.

THIS PAGE: *In this small, high-ceilinged guest room, I hung the wallpaper so that the stripes flowed horizontally, the better to expand the sense of space. The bed was designed to fit in the niche. I found the star on a trip to England.* OPPOSITE: *My clients had these paintings, which I named Ma and Pa, and they worked perfectly in this farmhouse guest room. The heart pine floor, beams, and low wainscot contrast effectively with the whitewashed boards, and contemporary spindle beds contribute to the country atmosphere.*

Rustic and refined elements provide a
mix of masculine and feminine, making
a space comfortable for everyone.

I like to keep accessories to a minimum in guest rooms, but my client's collection of "corn" majolica worked exceptionally well in this cheerful farmhouse guest room. Sunny yellow was the color of choice, appearing in the old-fashioned rag rug, curtains, and bed throw, as well as the sunflower-print pillows. The pom-pom bedspread, with its tasseled trim, finishes this simple, pleasing country picture.

Fresh flowers on a bedside table are the easiest, and least expensive, way to make a guest room say *welcome*.

THIS PAGE AND OPPOSITE: *The lyrical painting over the fireplace, by Atlanta artist Carolyn Carr, reminded me of music and inspired this guest room's design, which is quiet and soothing yet incorporates moments of lively detail. Drum pendant fixtures and asymmetrical cowhide rugs at either end of the room mark the sleeping and living zones. The milk chocolate walls serve as a monochromatic background for the subtle scrollwork on the bedspread and polka-dot chair pillows.*

THIS PAGE AND OPPOSITE: *Deep, rich navy blue works well in a guest room: It is enveloping and sleep-promoting, as well as unexpected. The space at right incorporates shades of navy and gray and gentleman's fabrics in a play on menswear. Above, I paired the blue walls with khaki and lots of striped and printed fabrics.*

THIS PAGE AND OPPOSITE:
These two identically shaped rooms were designed for sisters, and I wanted them to be alike yet different, so as to express the girls' contrasting personalities. Accordingly, I used the same components—platform beds, nightstands, vibrant patterns and colors—but gave each room its own character.

I often decorate siblings' rooms as mirror images of one another. There are no hard feelings, and when the kids move on, the guests slip in with ease.

THIS PAGE AND OPPOSITE: *This Nashville guest room is actually a freestanding "bunkhouse" with its own kitchenette and bathroom as well as two queen-size beds. I wrapped the walls in paisley and chose solid colors for the rest of the scheme. The animal heads above the beds are made of birch wood; the antique dresser, with its unusual Greek key motif, was found in England.*

Kids' Rooms

E very child needs a place in which to create the kind of happy memories that last a lifetime—that is the gold standard for success in kids' rooms. And while it can be very tempting to do so, it is unfair to children for parents to force them to live with an adult fantasy of the perfect young person's environment. Don't hide what's important to them, even if you don't like looking at it. Let them express themselves freely, and exempt their spaces from the "perfect house" tour. Kid-friendly—not adult-friendly—is the name of the game.

It has been my experience that kids only really see two things: the bed and—in particular—the shade of the walls. In fact, when it comes to decorating a child's room, the most important thing is color, color, color. I have had "design meetings" with lots of kids, and not a one has ever requested a beige room. In fact, all my young clients have proven quite decisive: When I put a bunch of color choices in front of them, they told me immediately what they liked, and I worked it into the walls, curtains, rugs, beds, and artworks, with brighter secondary colors for the door, trim, and ceiling.

The other important consideration regarding kids' rooms is practicality. Make sure there is abundant storage for toys and books. Choose rugs with patterns, the softest ones you can find, and maximize open floor space. Set the rods in the closets at an appropriate height. Conceal the television and computer wiring if possible to diminish clutter but also to make the room's eventual conversion to a guest space easier. Install more than one night-light, and desk lamps that encourage reading. And remember: Bunk beds are adorable, and kids love them, but they are super-hard to make up.

PREVIOUS: *The oversize head- and footboards on these twin beds generously showcase the medallion pattern on the upholstery. The walls are covered in an easy-to-clean lavender wallpaper that adds color, texture, and practicality.* OPPOSITE: *The artist Carson Fox hand-molded and painted each of these flowers, then pinned them to the wall, to create a site-specific sculpture—a cascade of flowers that is the first thing the girls see when they open their eyes in the morning.*

THIS PAGE AND OPPOSITE: *The white background in this beach house bedroom creates a restful backdrop for the swaths of vibrant color. The shell mirror and natural coral sculpture reference the location. And I have yet to meet a little girl who didn't love a white flokati-covered stool.*

THIS PAGE: *As in this room's sister space, shown on the previous pages, white surfaces support vibrant pops of color. The twin bed–size window seat (with storage drawers underneath) is perfect for sleepovers.* OPPOSITE: *I wanted this basement-level bunk room to promote napping, and so finished it in dark walls with richly hued trim—offset by lively patterns in the artwork and bedding.*

PREVIOUS: *This vibrant playroom for three little girls is also superpractical: The carpet is composed of individual squares that can be separately taken up and replaced as necessary.* OPPOSITE: *When this little girl expressed a preference for lavender, I took the color and ran with it. Despite the room's multiple comfortable spots (including the entirety of the soft shag rug), the child's favorite spot is the window seat—as you can jump up, pull the curtain, and have an instant cozy hideaway.*

THIS PAGE AND OPPOSITE: *As kids get older, the design of their rooms reflects their increasingly sophisticated tastes and needs. This colorful space, for a college-age young adult, features a king-size bed and a sofa bed for sleepovers—and will transition easily into a guest room once the nest is empty.*

White walls provide the backdrop for the jolts of turquoise and lime green in this room, which contains a bed and a daybed. An oversize monogram on the curtain valance personalizes the space.

THIS PAGE: *The patterned ceiling makes this small bedroom feel more spacious. I chose navy and khaki as my primary colors—because what little boy doesn't own a navy blazer and a pair of khaki pants?* OPPOSITE: *To give this room height, I extended the upholstered headboard to the ceiling and set the reading lights directly into it. The headboard also shapes a space within a space in the diminutive room, making it feel larger.*

Children's rooms should be durable, colorful, and stimulating. Much is expected of children in later years—so make them feel safe and special.

232

This room is so vibrant, it casts a glow into the adjoining hallway—you preview the space before you actually enter it. My custom-designed rug, with its abstract flower pattern and deep pile, offers an abundance of floor space on which to play, and the sofa and deep window seats comprise a veritable sleepover heaven. The curtained space between the windows is a favorite spot—complete with a reading lamp and curtains to ensure privacy.

234

Bathrooms

*J*im and I were married twenty-seven years ago. In our first house, we shared a tiny bathroom with one sink. It didn't matter then— we were so excited to be homeowners, and we were young. Many years later, we renovated a house and designed and built a proper bathroom, with two vanities, a separate tub and shower, and a water closet. That was a game changer. Jim was so relieved to get away from all my clutter, and I was so grateful for the space and a little privacy. As important as the master bedroom is to a couple, the master bath is equally critical.

Aesthetically, you want the space to relate to the bedroom, with which it typically communicates: They don't have to match, but the two rooms should reflect one another in terms of style and color. Assign the master bath enough square footage to let the two of you function together, and design the room so that it flows comfortably and encourages you and your spouse to freely move about the space.

From a decorative standpoint, the big story in the bathroom is tile design. Give full rein to your creative impulses—use shapes and colors to create patterns and borders. In a shower, to cite one example, I put 4-by-4-inch (10-by-10-cm) tiles on the floor, created a "wave" pattern on the walls, and applied 6-by-6-inch (15-by-15-cm) diagonal tiles to the ceiling—in addition to taking a fourth approach to the curb and using a solid slab in the bath-products niche. The cost is similar to that of doing everything the same way, and the outcome is far more original.

PREVIOUS: *The patterned tile beneath the chair rail extends into the shower and is balanced by the large solid-color tiles on the floor. I like bathroom shutters with louvers that are not too big and not too small.* OPPOSITE: *Freestanding tubs without feet are luxurious, tidy in appearance, and easy to keep clean. In the absence of a tub deck, a side table or garden seat holds bath products.*

The biggest mistake you can make in any bathroom, and the one I come across most frequently, is inadequate lighting. In my experience, you need three sources: makeup (or shaving) light in the form of sconces that flank the mirror (or a horizontal tubular fixture above it); recessed lights above the vanity; and a chandelier or pendant to produce even overall illumination. I especially like natural light in a bathroom. In fact, when checking in to a hotel, one of the first questions I always ask is whether or not my bathroom has a window. The benefits of natural light far outweigh the fact that you will need some sort of covering on the window to provide privacy. There are lots of options: shutters, 2-inch (5-cm) wood blinds, sheer café curtains, or sheer Roman shades with privacy shades beneath.

Some useful rules can help you get the space just right. The finishes on all the hardware, including the faucets, the knobs, and the tank lever, should match one another; the lighting and door hardware, however, can be different. Think about a luminous wall finish—it looks lively and fresh and cleans up easily. The minimum width for a double vanity is 76 inches (193 cm); if you cannot achieve an ideal depth of 36 inches (91 cm), use wall-mounted faucets—they will save you 3 inches (7.5 cm)—and an over-mirror light fixture rather than sconces flanking the mirror. Glass creates a fresh, clean feel in a bath: sandblasted, the material proves a good choice for shower doors and water closets, and back-painted glass provides the same effect but offers privacy for storage. I like to incorporate large mirrored medicine cabinets, but if your vanity drawers eliminate the need, decorative mirrors provide more options. A linen closet for towels, bath products, and accessories is essential. And if you have a pocket door between the bedroom and bath, install full-length mirrors on both sides.

Ironically, one of the best places in your home to make a big decorative statement is one of the smallest, least-visited spaces: the powder room. Their size and infrequency of use work in their favor. If you want to use a wildly expensive wall covering or tile, it's OK, because you won't need much of it. And if you get the urge to do something experimental, unexpected, or totally over the top, the powder room's the perfect place, as it does not need to tie in aesthetically to the rest of the house.

The contrast between the crisp ovals of the mirrors and the "wave" tile pattern behind them gives this bathroom its distinction. The clean lines and repeating regularity of the vanities reinforce the difference. In a narrow bathroom, wall-mounted faucets will give you three extra inches of counter space.

PREVIOUS: *Having decorated the adjoining master suite in shades of lavender and gray, I brought the colors into this otherwise black and white bathroom. The strongly geometric patterned tile floor contrasts nicely with the soft palette, and I like the rhythm of the alternating sandblasted glass cabinets and oval windows.* THIS PAGE AND OPPOSITE: *In the same space, matching vanities face one another, and a comfortable chaise, beneath the window, adds an overlay of relaxation to the room's functionality.*

Once a master bath has met your wants and needs, let luxury take over—and don't be afraid to mix masculine and feminine elements.

In this New York bathroom, slabs of honey onyx (continued onto the floor) introduce luxury via the use of an exotic material. Sandblasted glass doors with custom nickel borders provide additional distinction. I generally prefer hooks to towel bars— unless they are heated, as is the case here.

THIS PAGE AND OPPOSITE: *When possible and appropriate, I like to use decorative mirrors such as these modern Venetian glass examples, rather than medicine cabinets, and insets on cabinet doors instead of painted wood— for example, shagreen (left) or antique mirror (right). I am also partial to banks of small drawers, which provide additional storage in a minimum of space.*

Inset panels on vanity doors are a great place to get creative. Mirrors, lighting, tile, hardware—in a bathroom, every detail matters.

OPPOSITE: *My husband, Jim, designed this small bathroom all in white to make it seem more spacious, then used a strongly graphic tile floor, with a neutral border, to make a bold statement.* THIS PAGE: *Mahogany— an unexpected choice for a bathroom vanity—gives this small bathroom a special distinction.*

A graphic "area rug" made from patterns of tile or marble helps to define space, and makes a strong statement.

THIS PAGE: *The tall cabinets flanking the octagonal mirror in this guest bath are great for storage, and also provided an opportunity for unusual side-mounted lighting. The unity of material above opened the way for the strongly graphic floor.* OPPOSITE: *I converted a midcentury dresser into a vanity for this powder room, and combined a marble sink and top to give the impression of a single continuous material. I chose gold faucets here to pair with the drawer pulls.*

Powder rooms are not about practicality—they're the perfect place to indulge in an over-the-top fantasy.

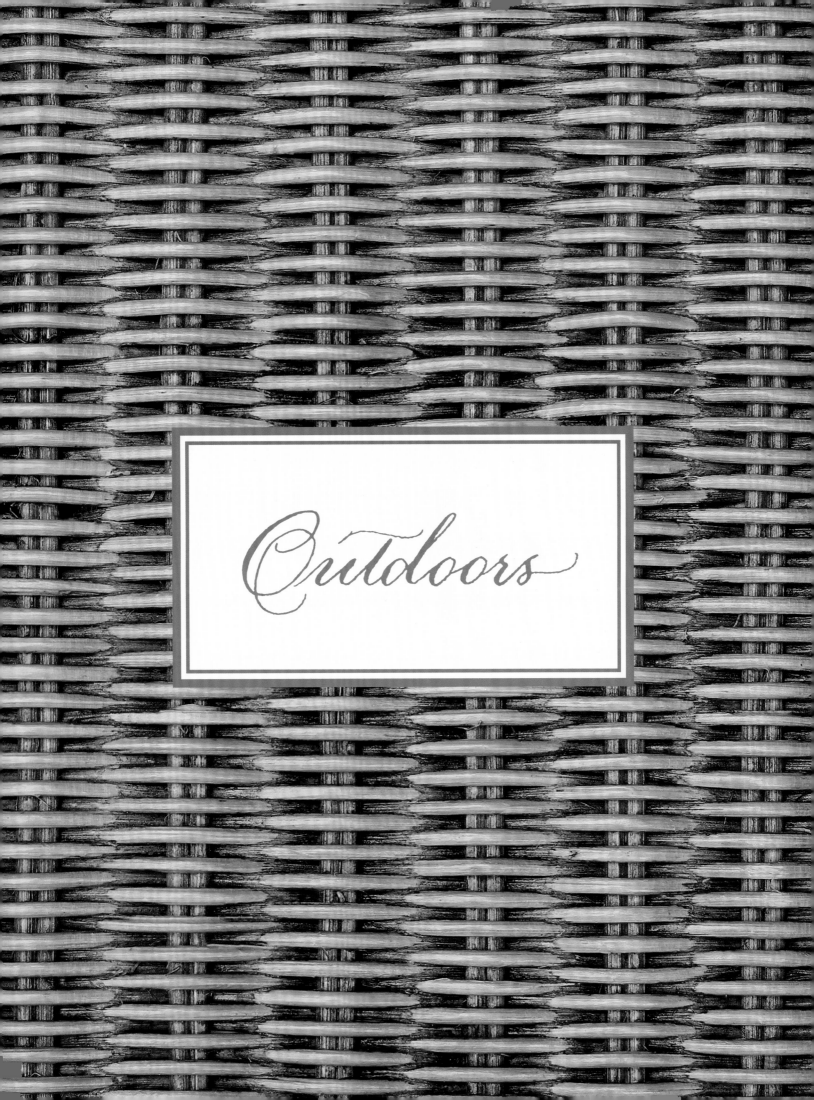

Outdoors

PREVIOUS AND THIS SPREAD: *There is something quintessentially Southern, in my view, about a screened porch—the sound of the door slamming shut always brings back memories—and this Sea Island back porch is no exception. The light wicker dining chairs are a nice contrast to the stone table and floor; as I don't like to use matching sets of everything, I selected a mix of fabrics and materials. I do, however, like to use indoor things in outdoor spaces—for example, the lamps.*

256

*I*n the South, we have the luxury of being able to use our outdoor spaces for most of the year, and we take advantage of it. To encourage my clients to do so, whenever possible I try to design outdoor living spaces that are extensions of the ones indoors. The more uses, the better: I like to incorporate places for lounging, conversing, dining, and just relaxing. I find that most of my clients prefer relaxing outdoors to dining, and so I work in as many different types of seating areas as I can. And, whenever possible, a swing or some rockers: All types of motion promote relaxation and add that extra layer of comfort.

Wood-burning outdoor fireplaces are probably my favorite thing in the world, and whenever I am decorating around one, I always make it a focal point—and make sure to get the right andirons, grills, and fireplace tools, as well as a great container to hold the wood. Even though you are out of doors, in the sunshine and breezes, be sure to carefully plan the lighting and fans. And make certain that there is adequate nighttime lighting, or you won't get as much use out of your outdoor spaces as you would like.

And though this might seem too obvious to mention, try to arrange things so that your outdoor rooms enjoy interesting and inviting views—if not long-distance vistas of nature or gardens, then a landscaped interior courtyard, or at the very least an interesting object or piece of architecture. You want your exteriors to be the perfect settings for welcoming friends and family—and having something good to look at will make them that much more irresistible.

This front porch in Nashville is notable for its multiple zones, which include chaise lounges, a dining table and chairs, and a rope swing; outdoor rugs help to define the different areas. The old-fashioned schoolhouse pendants and roll-up blinds give the porch a relaxed, easygoing quality—which is what outdoor spaces are all about, especially in the South.

PREVIOUS: *In my experience, outdoor living areas get more use than dining areas, and that has proven to be the case with this space, which is in the same house as the front porch pictured on page 259. A mix of patterns, and different table styles, sustain visual interest.* OPPOSITE: *Four black wicker chairs surround a circular stone ottoman in one of my favorite furniture arrangements—it is both inviting and spacious. The small side tables are made from resin.*

262

OPPOSITE: *Folding doors on both sides of a Charlotte, North Carolina, pool house open up the space to the views and the breeze. At this end of the room, a pair of one-arm chaises faces the television.*
THIS PAGE: *Chic lattice-back chairs surround an outdoor dining table.*

OPPOSITE AND THIS PAGE: *Two sets of four chairs in the same house—one grouping in the pool house, the other on a patio outside the breakfast room. I applaud architect Ken Pursley for his arrangement of multipurpose outdoor spaces in this pastoral setting.*

Four chairs, arranged in a circle around a table, make the perfect spot to relax outdoors with family and friends.

THIS PAGE AND OPPOSITE: *In this Birmingham garden, I opted to use a minimal amount of outdoor furniture—a pair of teak chaises with ceramic garden seats outside the pool house and a single bench—but the axial impact is precise and striking.*

ACKNOWLEDGMENTS

Writing a book is a complicated process; it takes months and months to lay it out and to write it, and luckily I have been working with some very talented professionals who have made the process so much easier for me. Doug Turshen, the man who has transformed the face of decorating books today, has taken the lead with this project, and his talents and working demeanor could not possibly improve. He just makes it easy; he truly has a natural talent. His right-hand man, Steve Turner, has added his creativity and tech savvy as well. Marc Kristal is a talented writer who somehow as a New York Jewish man managed to find the voice of an Irish girl from Alabama. Go figure . . . I thank Stewart, Tabori & Chang for taking another chance on me, and offering me the opportunity to make this vision a reality. Not to mention that they made the first book, *The Joy of Decorating*, a real hit! Thanks to my editor, Andrea Danese, for working tirelessly to see that everything is done properly.

The reality of this book and all the pretty pictures of the rooms that are shown in it are another story, however. There is nothing easy about selecting, ordering, and delivering all of the elements that go into a room to furnish it to meet and even exceed our clients' expectations. I have an incredible staff that does almost all of the work that is reflected here. There are so many layers of detail and tireless efforts involved: my project managers, the people who draw everything in CAD, the bookkeeping and accounting staff, the warehouse and delivery staff, and our cleaning staff all contribute irreplaceable skills and tireless effort, without which I would never be able to do what I do. I am truly grateful for my great employees. We have a Christmas party every year, and the running joke is that I say *please* and *thank you* in a speech at the party, and that it applies for the whole year! Well, I would like to say *please* and *thank you* here in the most meaningful way I possibly can to all of you for being so devoted, for making every day special, for making me laugh, and for being part of our work family.

I am extremely grateful to all of my fantastic clients, who have shown unlimited trust and confidence in me. Thank you for the opportunities you have given me, and for allowing me to share the pictures of your beautiful homes in this book. Everyone I meet is so interesting and such an inspiration to me. It has been a pleasure working for each and every one of you, and I look forward to all of our future projects together.

Lastly, I would like to thank two of our children, who have joined our business. Andrew, who has been working for twelve years, has become such a source of pride and joy for Jim and me. He has grown into a seasoned designer, with many happy clients and beautiful projects, which have captured the attention of national magazines, and hopefully soon, book editors as well. We are so proud and can't wait to see what his promising future brings. Nellie Jane, our daughter, has been with us for four years and has really lightened my daily life in a way that no one else could. Sons often go to work for their fathers, but daughters rarely go to work for their mothers. I am so lucky to be able to watch her talents unfold, and to watch her grow into the bright young design star that I know she will be one day. I can't wait to sit at one of her book signings, handing her the books and the pens! And most importantly, of course, thanks to my husband and business partner, Jim. You are my best friend, my sanity, and I could never do this without you. Thank you for your never-ending patience and guidance. You have been one hell of a husband to me, Jim.

PHOTOGRAPHY CREDITS

Jessie Preza, Pages: 2, 87, 90, 144, 174–175

Josh Gibson, Pages: 6, 10, 13, 16–17, 23, 29, 32–33, 40–41, 46–47, 48–49, 56–57, 58, 62, 68, 69, 76, 77, 78, 79, 91, 92, 93, 95, 100, 101, 102, 104, 105, 106–107, 113, 114, 116–117, 122, 124–125, 130–131, 132–133, 134–135, 138–139, 140–141, 142–143, 152, 153, 154–155, 156, 157, 158–159, 160, 176–177, 178, 180–181, 184, 185, 186–187, 188–189, 194, 204, 210, 220, 221, 222, 224–225, 226–227, 230–231, 232, 233, 234–235, 242–243, 244, 245, 248, 249, 252, 253

Lucas Allen, Pages: 15, 54, 55, 72, 73, 103, 161, 172, 179, 250, 251

Erica George Dines, Pages: 18, 19, 28, 94, 126–127, 128–129, 182, 183, 197, 200–201, 205, 206, 207, 208, 209

Maura McEvoy, Pages: 20, 21, 45, 64, 66, 164, 165, 193, 211, 216, 219, 241, 246–247

Lisa Romerein, Pages: 22, 74, 80, 83, 163

Tria Giovan, Pages: 24, 25, 38, 39, 42–43, 44, 67, 108, 109, 110–111, 112, 119, 120–121, 147, 166, 169, 170–171, 190, 191, 192, 198, 212, 213, 223, 262

Laurey W. Glenn/Southern Living, Pages: 26, 27, 50–51, 52, 53, 70, 71, 75, 84–85, 96–97, 98–99, 136–137, 148, 150, 151, 162, 202, 203, 214, 215, 228, 229, 236, 239, 254, 256–257, 259, 260–261

Ngoc Minh Ngo, Pages: 30, 34, 36

Stephen Young, Page: 61

Mike Carroll, Pages: 264, 265, 266, 267

Howard Lee Puckett, Pages: 268, 269

Published in 2015 by Stewart, Tabori & Chang
An imprint of ABRAMS

Copyright © 2015 Phoebe Howard

Library of Congress Control Number: 2014959142

ISBN: 978-1-61769-168-3

Editor: Andrea Danese
Designer: Doug Turshen with Steve Turner
Production Manager: Denise LaCongo

The text of this book was composed in Requiem.

Printed and bound in China

10 9 8 7 6 5 4 3 2 1

Stewart, Tabori & Chang books are available at special discounts when
purchased in quantity for premiums and promotions as well as fundraising
or educational use. Special editions can also be created to specification.
For details, contact specialsales@abramsbooks.com or the address below.

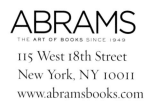

ABRAMS
THE ART OF BOOKS SINCE 1949

115 West 18th Street
New York, NY 10011
www.abramsbooks.com